BACKPACK 1

Second Edition

Mario Herrera · Diane Pinkley

Contributing Writer

Yoko Mia Hirano

PEARSON
Longman

Contents

Backpack Song

It's time to open **Backpack**
    and see what we can see.
We'll have lots of adventures.
Explore **Backpack** with me!

Backpack is full of fun things
    we use each day in school.
Stories, puzzles, songs, and games—
    Backpack is really cool!

It's time to open **Backpack**
    and see what we can see.
We'll have lots of adventures.
Explore **Backpack** with me!

Backpack is full of fun and facts,
    projects and pictures, too.
We're learning English, we're never bored.
There are great new things to do!

It's time to open **Backpack**
    and see what we can see.
We'll have lots of adventures.
Explore **Backpack** with me!

1 Ready for School

1 Listen and sing.

Hello!

Hello. I'm Ricky Red.
Look! I have one pen and
    I'm ready for school.

Hello. I'm Gracie Green.
Look! I have two books and
    I'm ready for school.

Hello. I'm Bobby Blue.
Look! I have three erasers and
    I'm ready for school.

Hello! Do you hear the bell ring?
It's time for school and
    we're ready to go!

red   green   blue

School supplies; colors

2 Look. Listen and say. Write.

What's your name?

My name is _____.

3 Count and say. Stick.

 one ◯   two ◯   three ◯   four ◯   five ◯

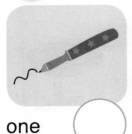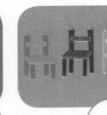

six ◯   seven ◯   eight ◯   nine ◯   ten ◯

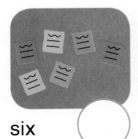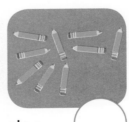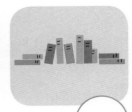

Unit 1

Greetings; numbers

3

TRACK A6

4 Listen and point. Listen and say.

1. backpack   2. book   3. chair   4. crayon   5. desk

6. marker   7. paper   8. pen   9. pencil   10. table

School supplies; verb *be*

5 Look at the picture. Point. Ask and answer.

What's this?

It's a backpack.

What color is it?

It's green.

Question formation; school supplies; contractions

Grammar

What**'s** this?　　It**'s** a chair.

6 Listen and circle.

1.

(pencil)　　　　eraser

2.

pen　　　　marker

3.

chair　　　　table

4.

backpack　　　book

5.

backpack　　　desk

6.

paper　　　　crayon

Questions with *be*; contractions

7 Look and listen. Say.

TRACK A10

8 Listen. Draw and color.

TRACK A11

It's a book.
It's red.

It's a crayon.
It's green.

Questions; verb *be*; contractions; colors

Unit 1

7

9 **Listen. Draw lines.**

1.

book

2.

chair

3.

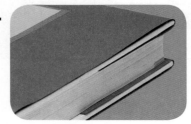

eraser

4.

pencil

10 **Listen and chant.**

Hey, Jill!

Hey, Jill!
What's this?
It's a pen, Bill.

Hey, Ken!
What's this?
It's a chair, Jen.

Hey, Matt!
What's this?
It's a table, Pat.

School supplies; rhythm and intonation

See Sound and Spelling Handbook p. 110

Make Color Groups

Draw and color. Use red, green, or blue.
Sort.

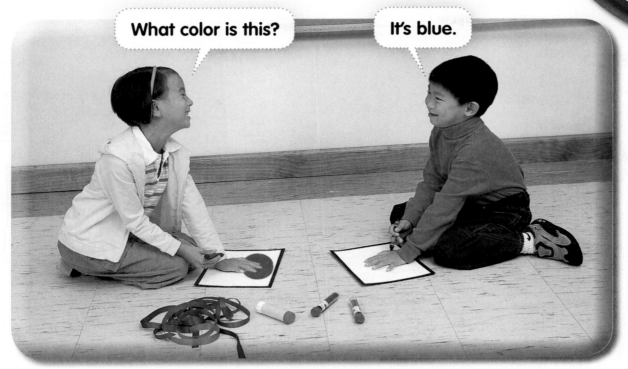

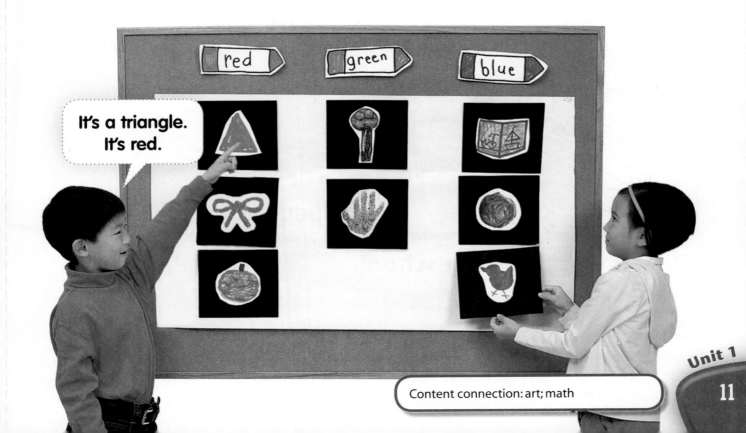

Content connection: art; math

Work Hard

Color.

Listen.

triangle

Read.

Write.

square

Speak.

Copy: I work hard in school.

Character education

Know It? Show It!

✓ Touch and guess.

What's this?

It's a crayon.

No.

It's a marker.

Yes.

Unit 1

I can do it!

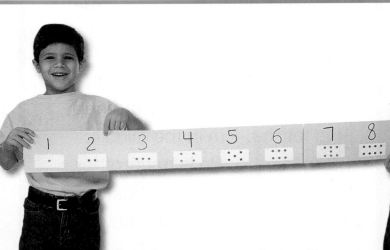

Make a number line.
Use the cutouts on
page 127.

Unit 1

13

Performance assessment
See Assessment Package pp. 23–25, 28, 37, 46–47.

② People We Love

TRACK A15

1 Listen and sing.

My Family Song

F is for Fred. He is my father.
A is for Ann. She is my mother.
M is for me. I'm in the middle.
I is for Isaac. He is my brother.
L is for Lucy. She is my sister.
Y is for Yoli. She is the baby.

F-A-M-I-L-Y. Put them all together.
They spell family.

F-A-M-I-L-Y. Put us all together.
This is my family!

14   Family members; alphabet

2 Look and listen. Point and say.

3 Stick and say.

Pam

Don

4 Listen and point. Listen and say.

1. father

2. mother

3. brother

4. sister

5. baby

6. grandfather

7. grandmother

8. parents

9. family

Family members; verb be

Jen

Tim

 TRACK A19

5 **Look at the picture. Ask and answer. Pretend.**

 TRACK A20

6 **Ask and answer about you.**

I have two sisters. Who am I?

You're Pam!

How many sisters do you have?

I have one sister.

Unit 2

Question formation; family members

17

How many brothers do you have?
I have **two** brothers.

 7 **Listen and color.**

TRACK A22

1.

2.

3.

 8 **Listen and circle. Say.**

TRACK A23

me

me

Questions with *how many*; verb *have*

TRACK A24

9 **Look and listen. Say.**

Who are they?

My two brothers.

Who is she?

She is my sister.

Hello! My name is Kim.

That is my sister!

TRACK A25

10 **Listen and draw.**

This is my family. Here's my mother and father. I have two sisters and one brother.

11 **Listen. Draw a line. Say the letters.**

1. two brothers

2. one sister

3. three sisters

12 **Listen and chant.**

Clap for Your Family

Sisters, sisters!
How many sisters do you have?
1, 2, 3
3 sisters. I have 3 sisters.
Clap for your sisters. 1, 2, 3

Brothers, brothers!
How many brothers do you have?
1, 2
2 brothers. I have 2 brothers.
Clap for your brothers. 1, 2

Family, family!
This is your family.
Clap for your family.
Clap for them all!

Family members; rhythm and intonation

See Sound and Spelling Handbook **p. 111**

Make an ABC Book

Draw and color.

C is for cat.

D is for desk.

Content connection: art; language arts

Love Your Family

Look and read. Act it out.

Play.

Hug.

Help.

Copy: I love my family.

24 Character education

Know It? Show It!

Spin and say.

Who are they?

They are my brothers.

How many brothers do you have?

Three.

Make a family picture. Use the cutout on page 129.

Look! This is my father.

Unit 2

I can do it!

Performance assessment
See Assessment Package pp. 23–25, 29, 38, 46–47.

3 Head to Toes

Look at Me!

Look at me! I'm in the ocean!
What do you see?
Two arms in the shape of a *V*.
Two arms in the shape of a *V*.

Look at me! I'm in the chair!
What do you see?
A big blue towel and long brown hair.
A big blue towel and long brown hair.

Look at me! I'm in the sand!
What do you see?
A white hat and just one hand.
A white hat and just one hand.

Look at me!

Parts of the body

2 **Look and listen. Say.**

| he | it | she | big | little | long | short |

1. She is <u>little</u>. **2.** She is <u>big</u>. **3.** He is <u>little</u>. **4.** He is <u>big</u>.

5. It is <u>short</u>. **6.** It is <u>long</u>.

3 **Listen and stick.**

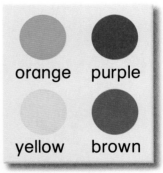

orange purple

yellow brown

It is big and brown.
It is long and orange.

It is little and yellow.
It is short and purple.

Unit 3

Subject pronouns; descriptive adjectives

27

4 **Listen and point. Listen and say.**

1. arm

2. ear

3. eye

4. hand

5. fingers

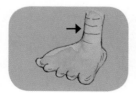
6. leg

7. mouth

8. nose

9. foot

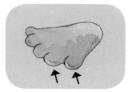
10. toes

Parts of the body; verb *have*

TRACK A34

5 **Look at the picture. Point. Ask and answer.**

> **Does it have long arms?**

> **Yes, it does.**

> **How many arms does it have?**

> **It has two arms.**

Unit 3

Question formation; verb *have*

29

Does she **have** a little mouth?   Yes, she **does**.

TRACK A36

6 **Look and listen. Check and say.**

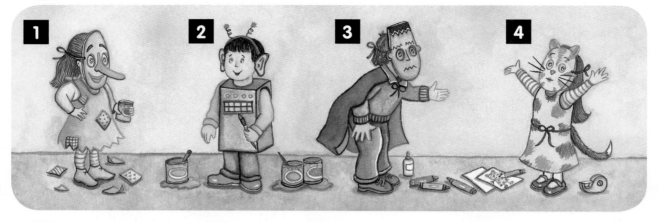

1   2   3   4

☐ yes   ☐ yes   ☐ yes   ☐ yes

☐ no   ☐ no   ☐ no   ☐ no

TRACK A37

7 **Look and listen. Point and count.**

Questions with third person singular; verb *have*

8 **Look and listen. Say.**

9 **Listen and draw.**

1

2

Subject pronoun *they*; verb *be*

10 Listen and check.

1.

2.

3.

4.

11 Listen and chant.

The Spider

How many eyes do you have?
I have eight—it's true! Do you?

How many legs do you have?
I have eight—it's true! Do you?

How many heads do you have?
I have one—it's true! Do you?

Parts of the body; rhythm and intonation

See Sound and Spelling Handbook p. 112

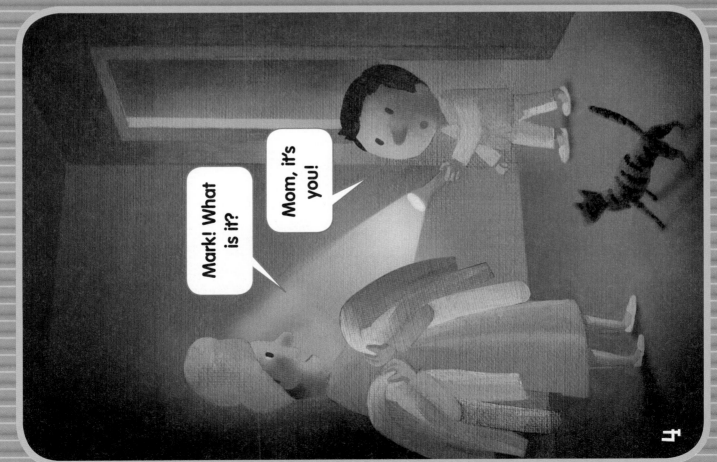

Are you scared, Tiger?
Let's look.

Mom! Dad! Help!
There's a monster in the hall!
It has a big head and seven arms!

Make a Surprise Drawing

Draw and fold. Take turns. Count.

Look at their drawing. There are three eyes, two ears, one nose, five arms, five hands, and four legs.

Content connection: art; math

Be Clean

Look and read. Circle.

Wash your **feet** / **hands**.

Wash your **nose** / **ears**.

Wash your **body** / **hair**.

Copy: I keep clean.

Character education

Know It? Show It!

Use the cutouts on page 131.
Match the creature cards.

My creature has two legs.

My creature has three legs.

My creature has three legs. It's a match!

Catch the ball. Talk about the creature poster.

Does it have green ears?

Yes, it does.

Unit 3
I can do it!

Performance assessment
See Assessment Package pp. 23–25, 38, 39, 46–49.

I Want Shoes

I'm wearing a jacket, a shirt, and pants,
   a shirt and pants.
I need one thing so I can dance.
So I can dance.

My jacket is blue, and my shirt is new.
My shirt is new.
My clothes are blue.
Now I want some shoes.

I'm wearing a jacket, a shirt, and pants.
I want some shoes so I can dance,
   so I can dance,
   so I can dance.

2 **Look and listen. Say.**

pink	white	black

3 **Stick and say.**

 TRACK A46

4 **Listen and point. Listen and say.**

1. dress   **2.** gloves   **3.** hat   **4.** jacket   **5.** pants

6. shirt   **7.** shoes   **8.** skirt   **9.** sneakers   **10.** socks

Clothing; singular/plural

 5 **Look at the picture.
Point. Ask and answer.**

 6 **Ask and answer
about you.**

**What is
he wearing?**

**He's wearing
green pants.**

**What are your
favorite clothes?**

**I like shirts
and pants.**

Question formation; present progressive;
simple present

Unit 4

41

Grammar

What **is** she **wearing**?   She**'s wearing** a white shirt.

7 **Listen. Draw a line. Color and say.**

1. She's wearing a green skirt.

2. He's wearing blue pants.

3. She's wearing a purple dress.

4. He's wearing a yellow jacket.

8 **Look and listen. Say.**

I have a sock.

I have a sock, too!

I have pants.

I have a shirt!

What are you wearing?

I'm wearing a big hat!

Questions with third, second person singular

9 Listen and circle.

1.

shoe   shoes

2.

hat   hats

3.

shirt   shirts

4.

sock   socks

10 Draw yourself. What are you wearing? Say.

Unit 4

11 Listen. Draw a line.

He's wearing blue pants.   She's wearing a purple dress.
He's wearing white shoes.   She's wearing a black jacket.
He's wearing a red T-shirt.   She's wearing a white hat.

12 Listen and chant.

What's This?

What's this?
    That's my new jacket.
    I'm going to pack it.

What's this?
    That's my blue sweater.
    It's for cold weather.

What's this?
    It's a pair of socks.
    Now throw away the box!

Clothing; rhythm and intonation

See Sound and Spelling Handbook
p. 113

The Fun House

by Mairead Stack

I'm going to
the summer fair.
I like to see what
people wear.

In the mirror, a boy
is laughing at me.
Look at him.
Who is he?

4

I'm walking in the big Fun House.

I see a girl in a funny yellow blouse.

I see a shirt. It's big. I see shoes. They're small.

In the mirror, the boy looks tall!

Make a Mobile

✂ Use the cutouts on page 133.
Talk about the clothes.

Art Project

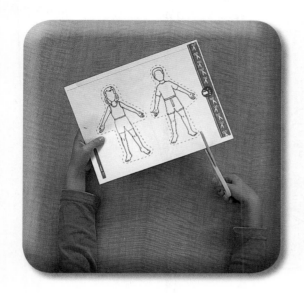

What is he wearing?

He's wearing a yellow shirt.

Content connection: art

Be Neat

Color.

Put away your clothes.

Copy: I am neat.

_____

Character education

Know It? Show It!

 TRACK A56 **Listen and color. Find three blue things in a row.**

Review

Make a collage of your favorite clothes.

I love hats!

Favorite Clothes

Unit 4
I can do it!

Performance assessment
See Assessment Package pp. 23–25, 31, 40, 46–47.

Let's Make a House!

*Let's make a house
    with paper and glue.
There's a project
    we can do.
Here are scissors.
Here's a pen.
Let's cut out shapes
    one to ten.*

Circles and squares
    all around.
Rectangles fall
    on the ground.

What's the shape
    that's left out?
"The triangle!"
    we both shout.

(Chorus)

circle   square   triangle   rectangle

Geometric shapes; arts and crafts

TRACK A58

2 **Listen. Look and count. Say.**

How many blue squares do you see?

I see four blue squares.

3 **Make a house. Stick. Show and say.**

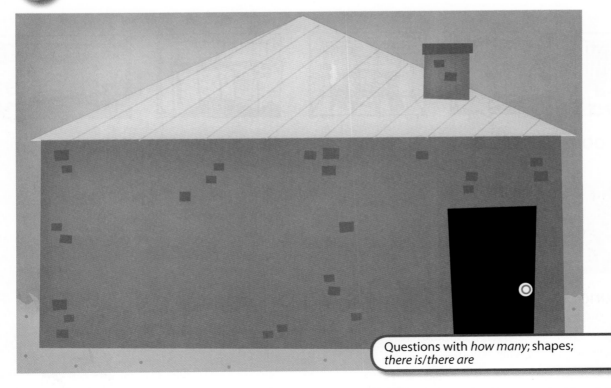

Questions with *how many*; shapes; *there is/there are*

Unit 5

51

4 Listen and point. Listen and say.

1. bathroom **2.** bedroom **3.** dining room **4.** kitchen **5.** living room

6. cooking **7.** eating **8.** reading **9.** sleeping **10.** watching TV

Rooms in a house; daily actions

⑤ Look at the picture. Point. Ask and answer.

> Where's the mother?

> She's in the living room.

> What's she doing?

> She's reading.

Question formation; simple present;
present progressive; contractions

Grammar

Where's your sister? She**'s** in the living room.

6 Look and listen. Write the number.

1

7 Circle the action that is different. Write it and say.

| cooking | eating | reading | sleeping | watching TV |

1. She's _____. She's _____. He's ___*eating*___.

2. She's _____. He's _____. He's _____.

3. She's _____. He's _____. She's _____.

54

Questions with *where*; contractions;
simple present; present progressive

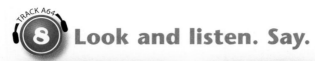

TRACK A64

8 **Look and listen. Say.**

9 **Color. Write and say.**

_____   _____

10 Listen. Draw lines.

1.

sleeping

2.

reading

3.

cooking

4.

watching TV

11 Listen and chant.

We Are Busy

She is sleeping.
She is sleeping.
Please don't shout.
Shh! Shh! Shh!

He is eating.
He is eating.
I'd like some.
Yum. Yum. Yum.

We are playing.
We are playing.
Let's have fun!
Fun! Fun! Fun!

Actions; present progressive; rhythm and intonation

See Sound and Spelling Handbook ➤ p. 114

Make a Fun Wheel

✂ Draw and cut. Spin and say.

 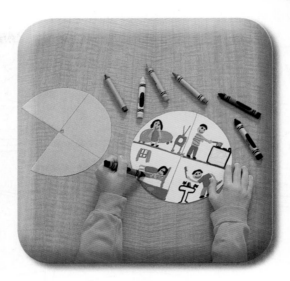

She's sleeping in the bedroom.

Content connection: art

Help at Home

Color.

Make your bed.

Clean the table.

Copy: I help at home.

Character education

Know It? Show It!

Cut out the house on page 135.
Listen and draw.

Draw a bed in room number 2.

This is my living room.

Make a room.

Unit 5

I can do it!

Performance assessment
See Assessment Package pp. 23–25, 32, 41, 46–47.

TRACK A68

1 Listen and sing.

All Around the Farm

A cow, a duck,
a great big truck!
A goat, a cat,
oh, look at that!

A horse, a hen,
chicks in a pen,
A dog, a rake,
an egg, a snake!

All around the farm,
what else can we see?
All around the farm,
take a look with me!

Ducks are swimming.
Sheep are eating.
Birds are flying.
Frogs are jumping.

(Chorus)

Farm animals

2 Look and listen. Say.

TRACK A69

> This is a frog.
> It's a big frog.

> This is a frog, too.
> It's a little frog.

3 Listen and stick. Say.

TRACK A70

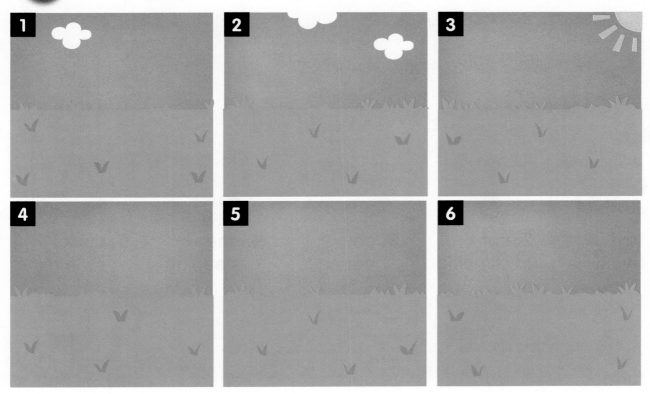

| 1 | 2 | 3 |
| 4 | 5 | 6 |

Hello.

4 Look and point. Listen and say.

1. bird flying
2. cat climbing
3. cow eating
4. dog sleeping
5. duck swimming

Hello.

6. farmer talking
7. frog jumping
8. horse running
9. sheep walking
10. worm crawling

Farm animals; action verbs

5 **Look at the picture. Point. Ask and answer.**

What are they?

They're sheep.

What are they doing?

They're walking.

Unit 6

Question formation; simple present; present progressive

65

What **is** the fish doing?   **It's** swimming.
What **are** the cows doing?   **They're** eating.

TRACK A75

6 **Look and listen. Draw a line.**

1.

2.

It's eating.

They're walking.

3.

It's jumping.

4.

It's flying.

5.

They're sleeping.

Present progressive; verb *do*;
singular/plural

TRACK A76

7 **Look and listen. Say.**

What is it?

It's a bird.

What are they?

They're frogs.

What are they doing?

They're jumping! Watch out!

TRACK A77

8 **Listen and draw.**

Questions; contractions; simple present; present progressive

Unit 6

67

9 **Look and write. Say.**

1.  They're _____.

2.  It's _____.

3.  They're _____.

4.  It's _____.

5. They're _____.

eating
flying
running
swimming
walking

10 **Listen and chant.**

TRACK A78

Look and See!

This is fun.
Look and see!
The birds are dancing.
They're dancing with me.

This is fun.
Look and see!
The birds are flying.
They're flying with me!

68 Present progressive; singular/plural; rhythm and intonation

See Sound and Spelling Handbook p. 115

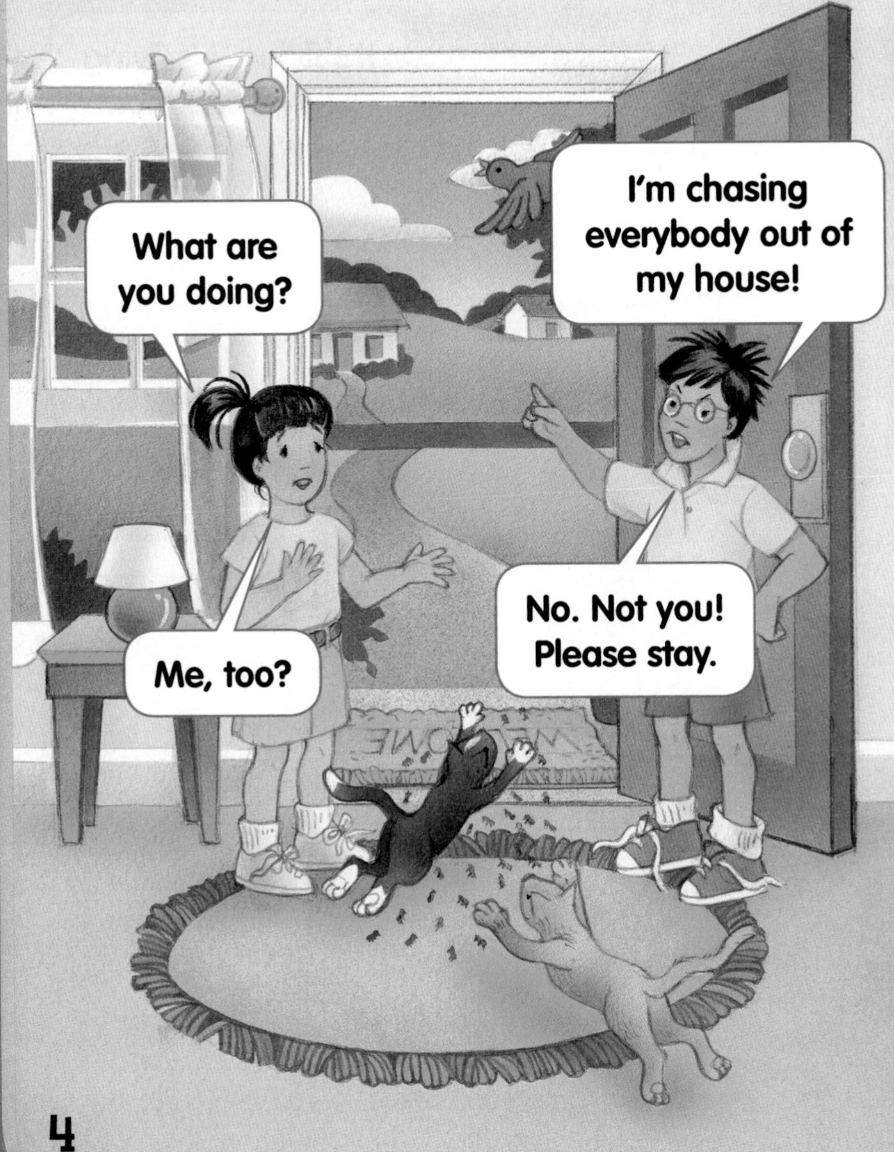

Out of My House!

by Yoko Mia Hirano

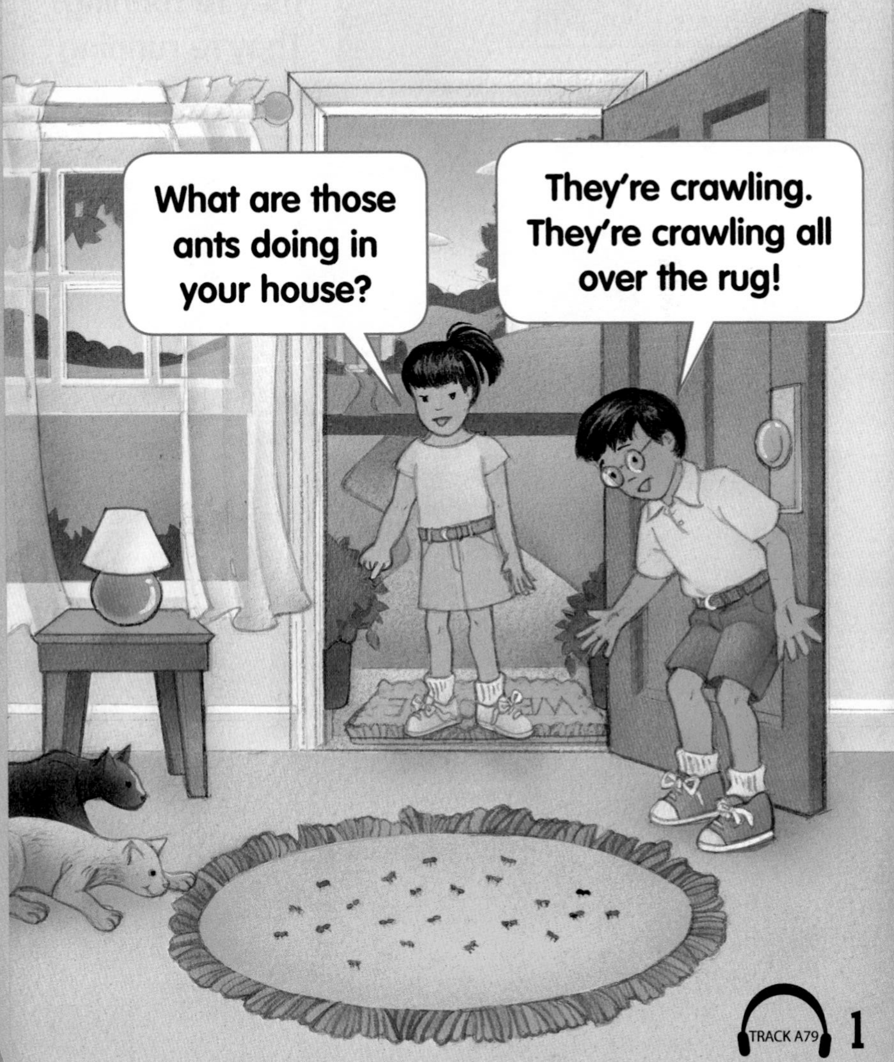

TRACK A79

What are those cats doing?

They're running. They're running after the ants.

What is that bird doing?

It's flying. It's flying all over the room.

Make Animal Puppets

✂ Color and cut out the animals on page 137.

Here's a little turtle and a big horse.

The turtle is my pet. The horse is on a farm.

Unit 6

71

Content connection: science; art

Take Care of Your Pet

Draw a line from the word to the pet.

Play with your pet.

Brush your pet.

cat
dog
fish
hamster

Feed your pet.

Clean up after your pet.

Copy: I take care of my pet.

Character education

Know It? Show It!

Look and say.

What are the horses doing?

They're eating.

1.

2.

3.

4.

5.

6.

7.

8.

Play charades.

You're a frog.
You're jumping.

Unit 6

I can do it!

Performance assessment
See Assessment Package pp. 23–25, 33, 42, 46–47, 50–51.

7 Celebrations

1 Listen and sing.

A Happy Day

Tuesday is my birthday
* and it will be a happy day.*
Tuesday is my birthday.
I'll have a party to celebrate.

I want pizza, lemonade, and cake,
  or some ice cream and a nice
  milk shake.
I want hot dogs and an apple pie,
  and lots of birthday gifts
  piled high.

(Chorus)

Party food

2 Look and listen. Say.

3 Listen and say. Listen and stick.

 TRACK B5

4 Listen and point. Listen and say.

1. cake

2. fish

3. hamburgers

4. ice cream

5. lemonade

6. milk

7. juice

8. pizza

9. rice

10. salad

11. sandwiches

Party food

5 Look at the picture. Point. Ask and answer.

6 Ask and answer about you.

What does he have?

He has lemonade.

Do you like lemonade?

Yes, I do.

Unit 7

Question formation; verbs *have, like*

77

Grammar

What **does she have**?   **She has** cake.
What **do you have**?   **I have** cake.

 7 **Look and listen. Circle.**

1. She has

cake.   **a hamburger.**

2. I have

a hot dog.   **pizza.**

3. He has

two hot dogs.   **two presents.**

4. He has

pizza.   **a sandwich.**

5. I have

milk.   **lemonade.**

6. She has

three balloons.   **three hats.**

78

Simple present; third, second, first person
singular of *have*

8 Look and listen. Say.

9 Listen and draw.

TRACK B11

I have salad, pizza, and orange juice.

Questions with *have*; first, second, third person singular; food

10 Listen and write.

| cake | ice cream | milk | rice | salad |

1. I have _____ on Monday.

2. I have _____ on Tuesday.

3. I have _____ on Wednesday.

4. I have _____ on Thursday.

5. I have _____ on Friday.

11 Listen and chant.

A Celebration

Today I have a present.
It's little, blue, and round.
It's for a celebration,
    and it makes a funny sound!

Today I have a present
    in a box that's green and square.
It's for a celebration.
It's something I can wear!

Today I have a present.
Whatever can it be?
It's for a celebration.
Come, open it with me!

Food; rhythm and intonation

See Sound and Spelling Handbook p. 116

Rabbit Joe Has a Party

by Yoko Mia Hirano

Rabbit Joe is planning a party.

Rabbit Sue says he needs pizza, cake, and ice cream.

Many rabbits come to the party.

Rabbit Joe has carrot soup and lettuce pie.

He does not need pizza, cake, or ice cream!

Rabbit Joe has a garden with vegetables.

He does not have pizza, cake, or ice cream.

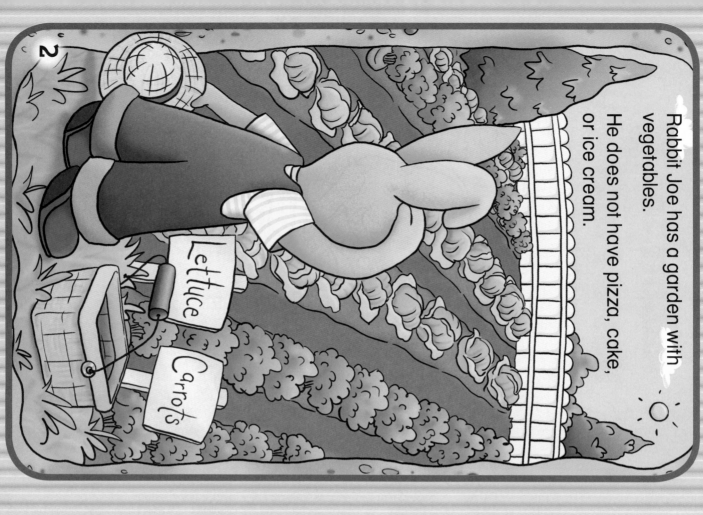

Rabbit Joe has carrots and lettuce.

He loves to eat vegetables.

Time for Presents

Art Project

✂ Cut out the present on page 139.
Cut and tape. Draw and say.

What do you have?

I have a computer game.

Content connection: art

Celebrate Special Days

Color.

Father's Day

Christmas

Birthday

Copy: I celebrate special days.

Character education

Know It? Show It!

Make a food pocket game.

Is it a hot dog?

Guess the Food

Yes, it is.

Do you like hot dogs?

Yes, I do.

Draw your favorite foods.

My favorite foods are fish and oranges.

Unit 7

I can do it!

Performance assessment
See Assessment Package pp. 23–25, 34, 43, 46–47.

Toy Box

The Toy Box

I have a toy box, big and brown.
I look inside and find a clown.
I have a toy box with twelve toys,
    some toys for girls,
    some toys for boys.

Clap your hands!
Clap your hands!
I play all day with my toy box.

I have a toy box. I look inside.
I see it's empty—now I can hide!

(Chorus)

Toy Box

1 2 3 4 5 6 7 8 9 10 11 12

Toys; equipment

2 **Look and listen. Say.**

in
on
under

Where is the crayon?

It's on the book.

3 **Count and say. Stick.**

eleven

twelve

thirteen

fourteen

fifteen

sixteen

seventeen

eighteen

nineteen

twenty

Unit 8

4 Listen and point. Listen and say.

1. bikes

2. blocks

3. boats

4. dolls

5. kites

6. marbles

7. planes

8. skates

9. trains

10. yo-yos

Toys; equipment; plural forms

TRACK B19

5 Look at the picture. Point. Ask and answer.

What does she want?

She wants some blocks.

Where are the blocks?

They're on the shelf.

Question formation; verb *want*;
prepositions of location

What do you want?

I want a ball.

bike
book
car

TRACK B21

6 Listen and write. Draw a line.

1. I want a blue _____.

2. I want a red _____.

3. I want a green _____.

Grammar

Where's the ball?   It's **in** the toy box.

TRACK B22

7 Listen and circle. Draw a line.

1. The ball is **on** / **under** the chair.

2. The kite is **on** / **in** the toy box.

3. The doll is **under** / **on** the table.

90

Toys; verb *want*; prepositions of location

8 Look and listen. Say.

9 Draw and write.

The _____ is in the toy box.

The _____ is on the toy box.

10 **Look and listen. Write the number.**

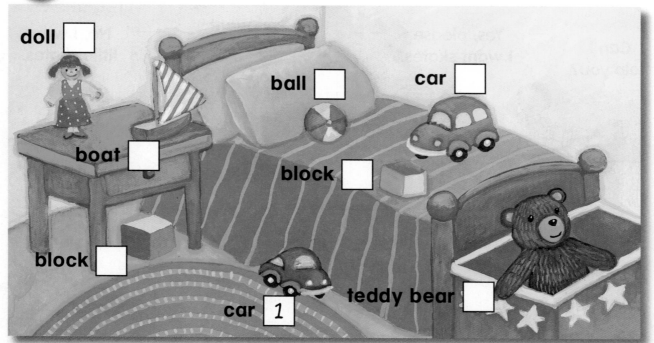

doll ☐

ball ☐ car ☐

boat ☐

block ☐

block ☐

car 1

teddy bear ☐

11 **Listen and chant.**

Where Is the Boat?

Where is the boat?
The boat is on the block.
The boat is on the block.

Where is the block?
The block is on the bike.
The block is on the bike.

Where is the bike?
The bike is rolling away!
Oh, no! Oh, no! Oh, no!

Oh, no! Oh, no! Oh, no!

Toys; prepositions of location; rhythm and intonation

See Sound and Spelling Handbook p. 117

Where's My Bear?

by Yoko Mia Hirano

I say, "I want my teddy bear.
Where is it, Dad?"

He says, "We'll look for it.
Don't be sad."

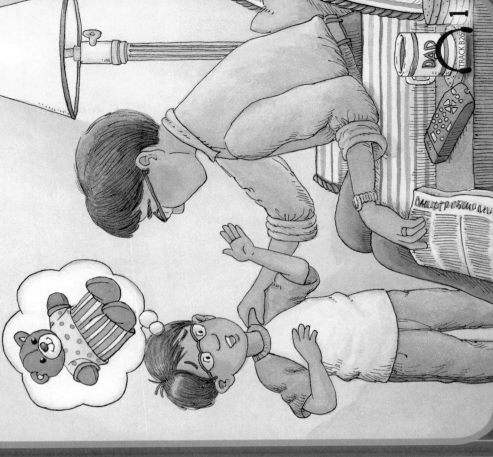

I say, "Oh, I see.
Maria likes my teddy bear.
I think that I'll just leave him there."

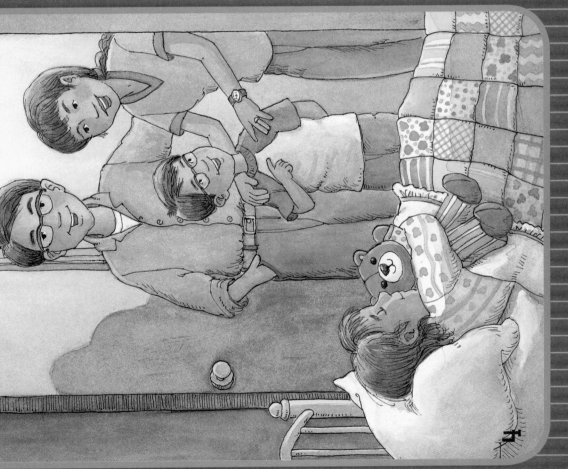

4

I say, "I want my teddy bear. It is red."
I look on my desk, and I look under my bed.

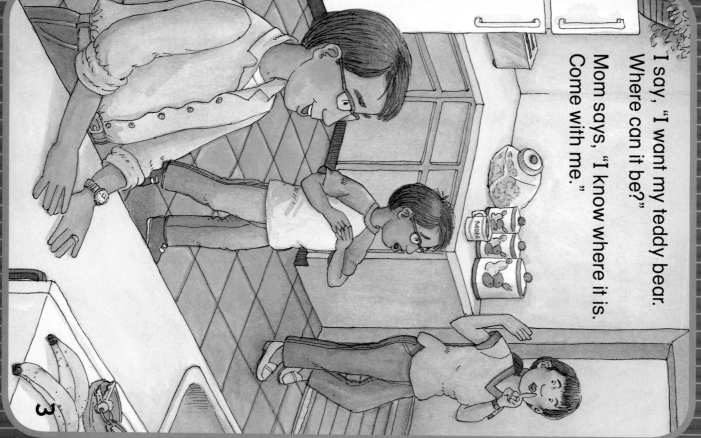
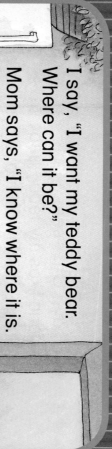

I say, "I want my teddy bear. Where can it be?"
Mom says, "I know where it is. Come with me."

Make a Toy Box

✂ Cut out the toy box label on page 141.

What's in your toy box?

I have a plane in my toy box.

Share with Others

What toys do you share? Circle the toys.

Share with your friends.

Copy: I share my toys.

Character education

Know It? Show It!

Look. Ask and answer.

What do you want?

I want a balloon.

you

she

he

you

she

he

she

you

Say where each toy is.

Unit 8

I can do it!

The ball is on the desk.

Performance assessment
See Assessment Package pp. 23–25, 35, 44, 46–47.

Unit 8

97

9 At the Playground

TRACK B27

1 Listen and sing.

Having Fun

We're at the playground.
We're kicking a ball.
We're dancing around.
Come and join us all!

We're taking a walk.
We're having a snack.
We're stopping to talk.
Put down your backpack!

We're having fun!
We're having fun!

We're singing a song.
We're flying a kite.
We're marching along
   from morning till night!

(Chorus)

98   Outdoor activities

TRACK B28

2 Look and listen. Point and say.

This bicycle is red.

That bicycle is blue.

These books are yellow.

Those books are green.

 TRACK B29

3 Listen and stick. Say.

This yo-yo is pink.
These planes are purple.

That ball is brown.
Those skates are red.

Demonstrative adjectives; colors

TRACK B31

4 **Listen and point. Listen and say.**

1. catching

2. dancing

3. eating

4. kicking

5. singing

6. throwing

7. jumping rope

8. playing a game

9. riding a bike

10. roller skating

Outdoor activities

5 Look at the picture. Point. Ask and answer.

Is he jumping rope?

No, he isn't.

Is he singing?

Yes, he is.

Question formation; present progressive

Grammar

Is she **singing**?   No, she **isn't**.
Is she **dancing**?   Yes, she **is**.

 6 **Look and listen. Read and circle.**

1. Is she catching a ball?

Yes, she is.   (No, she isn't.)

2. Is he kicking a ball?

Yes, he is.   No, he isn't.

3. Is she sleeping?

Yes, she is.   No, she isn't.

4. Is she jumping rope?

Yes, she is.   No, she isn't.

5. Is he throwing a ball?

Yes, he is.   No, he isn't.

6. Is he roller skating?

Yes, he is.   No, he isn't.

Yes/no questions; short answers

7 Look and listen. Say.

8 Listen and draw.

One boy is jumping rope.
Two girls are kicking a ball.

9 **Listen and write. Draw a line. Color.**

1. She's _____ a ball.

2. He's _____ rope.

3. She's _____ a bike.

4. He's _____ a ball.

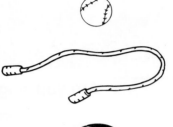

10 **Listen and chant.**

Kicking, Singing, Skating

He's kicking.
He's kicking.
He's kicking a ball.

She's singing.
She's singing.
She's singing a song.

He's skating.
He's skating.
Watch out. Don't fall!

Present progressive; rhythm and intonation

See Sound and Spelling Handbook

p. 118

Tony Is Reading

by Penny Young

TRACK B39

Tina says, "Tony, let's go to the playground."

Tony says, "I'm reading."

Tina says, "You can read at the playground."

Tony is catching at the playground.

And he's reading, too.

He's having fun!

Tony is swinging at the playground.
And he's reading, too.

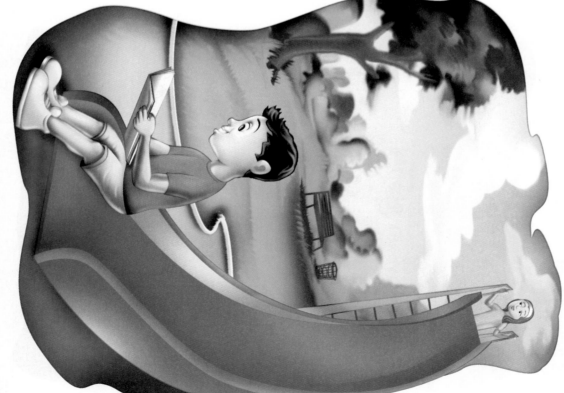

Tony is sliding at the playground.
And he's reading, too.

Make Action Puzzles

✂ Draw and color. Cut. Show and say.

She's riding a bike. She's skating. He's kicking a ball.

Content connection: art

Be Healthy

Look and read. Act it out.

Play soccer.

Jump rope.

Swim.

Ride a bike.

Copy: I get exercise.

Character education

Know It? Show It!
Look and say.

Review

Use cutouts on page 141.

These skates are green.
I want these skates.

This train is blue.
I want this train.

My Toy Shop

Unit 9
I can do it!

Unit 9
109

Performance assessment
See Assessment Package pp. 23–25, 36, 45–47, 52–53.

TRACK B40

1 Listen and say.

TRACK B41

2 Listen and say. Point to the picture below.

TRACK B42

3 Listen and say. Write the letter.

1 ___pple

2 ___ish

3 ___at

4 ___ird

5 ___ame

6 ___at

7 ___lephant

8 ___og

TRACK B44

1 Listen and say.

 TRACK B45

2 Listen and say. Point to the picture below.

 TRACK B46

3 Listen and say. Write the letter.

1 ___ce cream

2 ___onkey

3 ___encil

4 ___ite

5 ___urse

6 ___ion

7 ___acket

8 ___ueen

9 ___range

TRACK B48

1 Listen and say.

TRACK B49

2 Listen and say. Point to the picture below.

TRACK B50

3 Listen and say. Write the letter.

1
___iolin

2
fo___

3
___andwich

4
___o-yo

5
___mbrella

6
___able

7
___obot

8
___ebra

9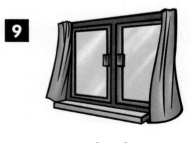
___indow

Sound and Spelling Handbook   *p* as in *pen*

TRACK B52

1 Listen and say.

TRACK B53

2 Listen and say. Point to the picture.

1  **2**  **3**  **4**

TRACK B54

3 Listen. Which words have the same sound as the *p* in *pen*? Circle the number.

1  **2**  **3**  **4**

4 Read. Underline the words with the same sound as the *p* in *pen*.

> This is my puppet. Her name is Pat. She has a pink shirt and purple pants. I like to play with Pat in the park.

5 What is in your backpack? Write words that have the same sound as the *p* in *pen*. Say.

_____

_____

1 Listen and say.

2 Listen and say. Point to the picture.

1    **2**    **3**    **4**

3 Listen. Which words have the same sound as the *e* in *bed*? Check the boxes.

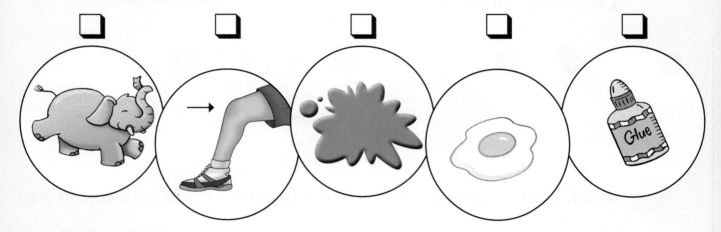

4 Read. Underline the words with the same sound as the *e* in *bed*.

This is my brother Ken. He's ten. He likes yellow shirts and shoes. His favorite drink is lemonade.

5 Look around you. Write words that have the same sound as the *e* in *bed*. Say.

_____

_____

1 Listen and say.

2 Listen and say. Point to the picture.

1    **2**   **3**    **4**

3 Listen. Which words have the same sound as the *r* in *red*? Trace the shapes.

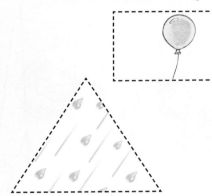   

4 Read. Underline the words with the same sound as the *r* in *red*.

This is grandfather's farm. His two horses are Brownie and Star. They are running to the river to drink water.

5 Write letters to make words with the same sound as the *r* in *red*. Say.

I have a new __ed __obot. It's a bi__thday p__esent

from my siste__ Ma__ia. My pa__ty was fun!

TRACK B61

1 Listen and say.

TRACK B62

2 Listen and say. Point to the picture.

1  **2**  **3** **4**

TRACK B63

3 Listen. Which words have the same sound as the *b* in *ball*? Check the stars.

4 Read. Underline the words with the same sound as the *b* in *ball*.

Billy is my baby brother. He likes to bounce his big blue and white ball. He likes to play in his bedroom.

5 Write words that have the same sound as the *b* in *ball*. Say.

two animals: _____

two rooms in a house: _____

TRACK B64

1 Listen and say.

TRACK B65

2 Listen and say. Point to the picture.

1    **2**    **3**    **4**

TRACK B66

3 Listen. Which words have the same sound as the *a* in *bat*? Connect the pictures.

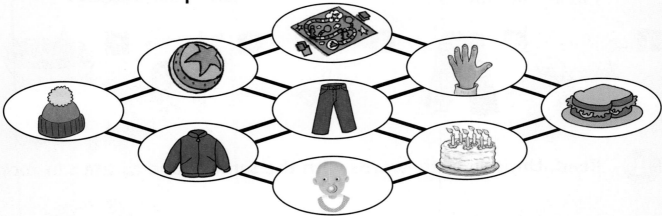

4 Read. Underline the words with the same sound as the *a* in *bat*.

Oh, no! There's a happy ant on my sandwich. And there are more ants walking on my salad, my apple, and my cake!

5 Write words that have the same sound as the *a* in *bat*. Say.

 _____

 _____

 _____

1 Listen and say.

TRACK B67

2 Listen and say. Point to the picture.

1    **2**    **3**    **4**

3 Listen. Which words have the same sound as the *s* in *sock*? Circle the number.

1    **2**   **3**   **4**   **5**

4 Read. Underline the words with the same sound as the *s* in *sock*.

> My sister Sonia is having a birthday party on Saturday. She will be seven. Sonia wants lots of presents!

Happy Birthday

5 Write words that have the same sound as the *s* in *sock*. Say.

two kinds of clothes: _____

two days of the week: _____

A   a B   b C   c

D   d E   e F   f

G   g H   h I   i

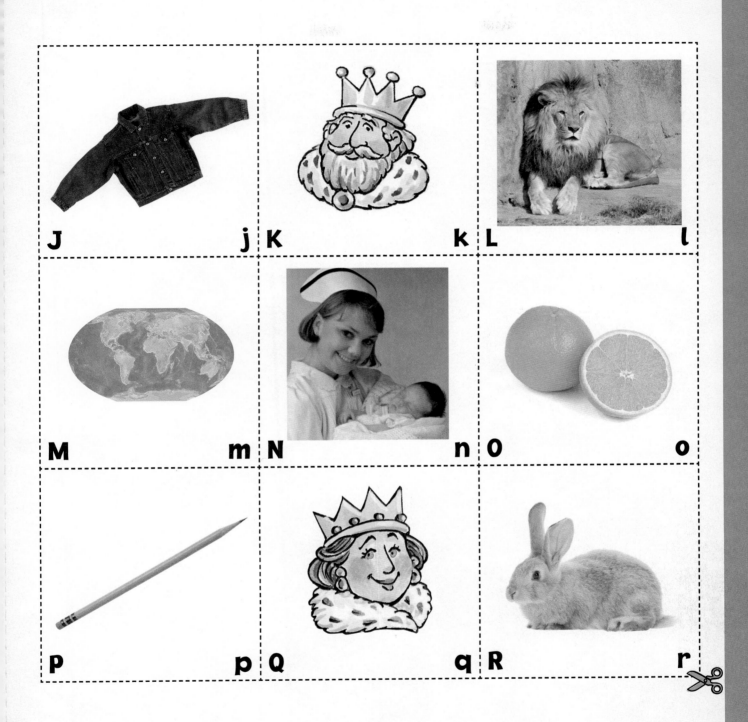

J   j K   k L   l

M   m N   n O   o

P   p Q   q R   r

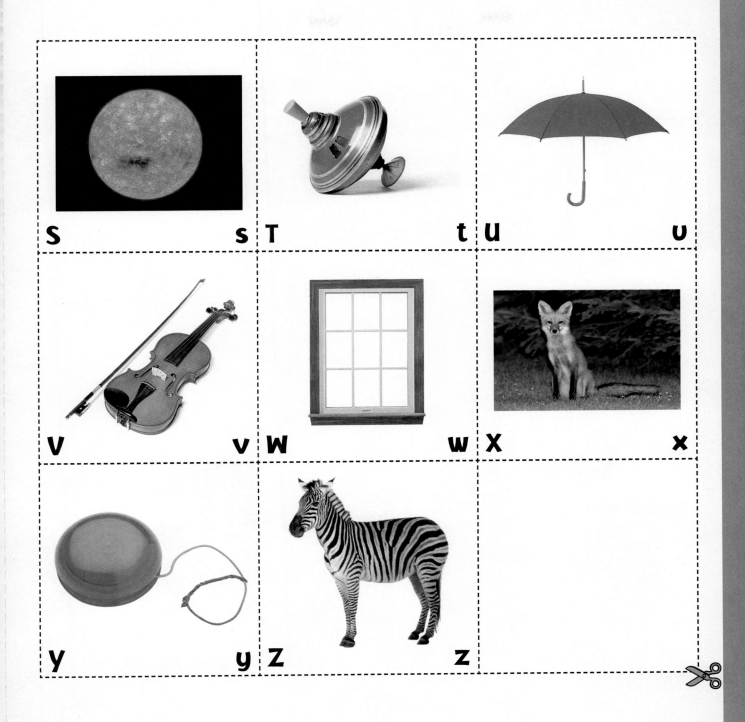

S s T t U u

V v W w X x

Y y Z z

Grammar and Writing

Subject Pronouns

I

you

he

she

it

we

you

they

Simple Present of *Be*

I am	we are
you are	you are
he is	
she is	they are
it is	

I am six.

She is 6 today.

Present of *Have*

I have	we have
you have	you have
he has	
she has	they have
it has	

I have ice cream.

He has ice cream.

Present Progressive

I'm walking	we're walking
you're walking	you're walking
he's walking	
she's walking	they're walking
it's walking	

I'm walking to school.

They're walking to school too.

Questions with *Be*
Yes/No Questions

Are you 6?

No, I'm 7.

Is she your sister?

Yes, she is.

Information Questions

Where's your doll?

What are they?

They're frogs.

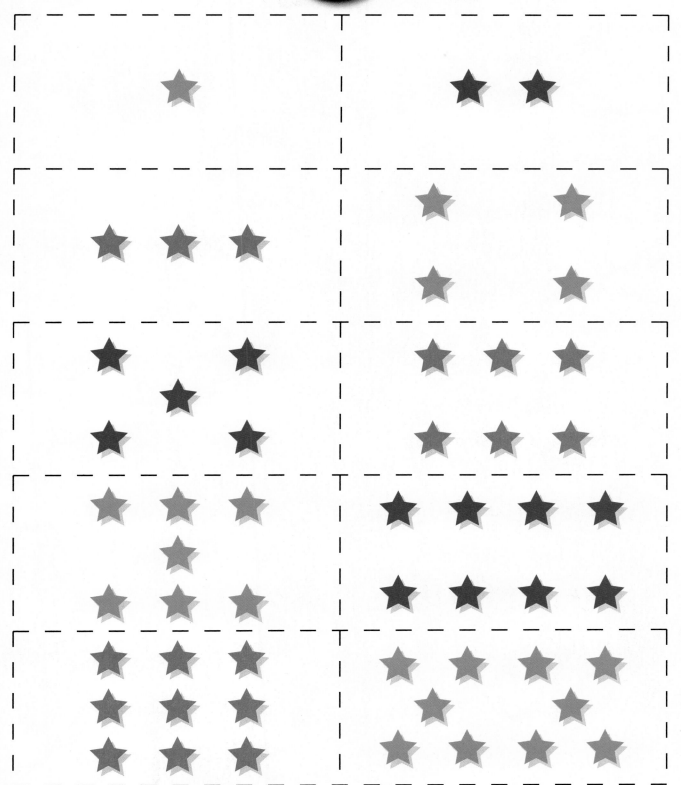

127

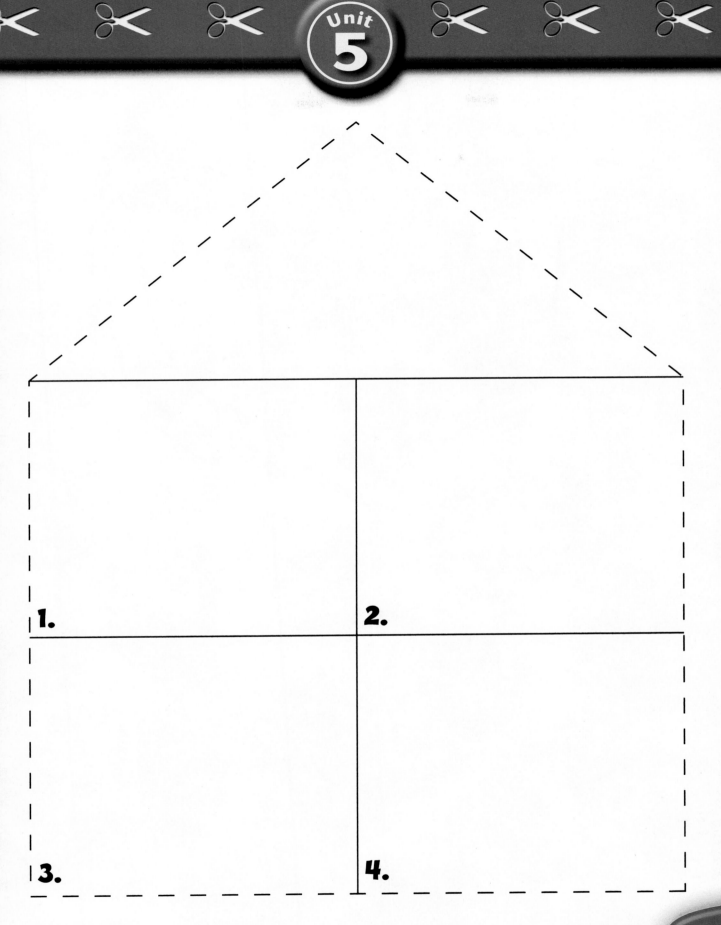

1.

2.

3.

4.

Unit
8

_____ 's

Toy Box

Unit
9